SandCastle

What Should I Eat?

Fruits
Are Fun

Amanda Rondeau

Consulting Editor
Monica Marx, M.A./Reading Specialist

ABDO
Publishing Company

Published by SandCastle™, an imprint of ABDO Publishing Company, 4940 Viking Drive, Edina, Minnesota 55435.

Printed in the United States.

Credits
Edited by: Pam Price
Curriculum Coordinator: Nancy Tuminelly
Cover and Interior Design and Production: Mighty Media
Photo Credits: Comstock, Corbis Images, Image 100, Image Source, PhotoDisc

Library of Congress Cataloging-in-Publication Data

Rondeau, Amanda, 1974-
    Fruits are fun / Amanda Rondeau.
      p. cm. -- (What should I eat?)
    Summary: A simple introduction to the fruit group of foods and why fruits are important for us to eat.
    ISBN 1-57765-834-5
     1. Fruit--Juvenile literature. 2. Nutrition--Juvenile literature. [1. Fruit. 2. Nutrition.] I.
    Title.

TX557 .R56 2002
641.3'4--dc21
                                                                                    2002018366

SandCastle™ books are created by a professional team of educators, reading specialists, and content developers around five essential components that include phonemic awareness, phonics, vocabulary, text comprehension, and fluency. All books are written, reviewed, and leveled for guided reading, early intervention reading, and Accelerated Reader® programs and designed for use in shared, guided, and independent reading and writing activities to support a balanced approach to literacy instruction.

Let Us Know

After reading the book, SandCastle would like you to tell us your stories about reading. What is your favorite page? Was there something hard that you needed help with? Share the ups and downs of learning to read. We want to hear from you! To get posted on the ABDO Publishing Company Web site, send us email at:

sandcastle@abdopub.com

SandCastle Level: Transitional

What is the fruit group?

Fats & Sweets
Eat LESS

MILK Group
2-3
servings

PROTEIN Group
2-3
servings

VEGETABLE Group
3-5
servings

FRUIT Group
2-4
servings

GRAIN Group 6-11 servings

*For suggested serving sizes, see page 22.

This is the food pyramid.

There are 6 food groups
in the pyramid.

The food pyramid helps us
know how to eat right.

Eating right helps us
stay healthy.

The fruit group is part of the food pyramid.

We should eat 2 to 4 servings of fruit every day.

Fruits are good for our bodies.

There are many kinds of fruit in the fruit group.

Fruit gives us many vitamins that we need.

Fruit helps us stay strong.

Did you know apples are fruit?

Apples come in different colors.

They are red or yellow or green.

Apples are a good snack.

Did you know strawberries are fruit?

Each strawberry has about 200 seeds.

Strawberries are good on cereal for breakfast.

Did you know raisins are fruit?

Raisins are dried grapes.

Raisins are sweet and make a great dessert after lunch.

Did you know bananas are fruit?

Bananas have been grown for over 1 million years.

Bananas are soft and good in smoothies.

Can you think of other foods in the fruit group?

What is your favorite food in the fruit group?

Index

What Counts As a Serving?

Fruit		
1 medium apple, banana, or orange	½ cup of chopped, cooked, or canned fruit	¾ cup of fruit juice

Glossary

breakfast the first meal after you wake up in the morning

dessert a sweet food, like fruit or ice cream, served after a meal

fruit the fleshy, usually sweet, part of a tree or plant grown for food

healthy to be well, also doing things that keep us well

serving a single portion of food

vitamins a substance that we need for good health, found naturally in plants and meats

About SandCastle™

A professional team of educators, reading specialists, and content developers created the SandCastle™ series to support young readers as they develop reading skills and strategies and increase their general knowledge. The SandCastle™ series has four levels that correspond to early literacy development in young children. The levels are provided to help teachers and parents select the appropriate books for young readers.

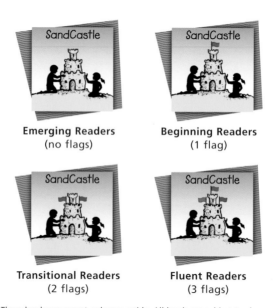

Emerging Readers
(no flags)

Beginning Readers
(1 flag)

Transitional Readers
(2 flags)

Fluent Readers
(3 flags)

These levels are meant only as a guide. All levels are subject to change.

To see a complete list of SandCastle™ books and other nonfiction titles from ABDO Publishing Company, visit www.abdopub.com or contact us at:

4940 Viking Drive, Edina, Minnesota 55435 • 1-800-800-1312 • fax: 1-952-831-1632